wiping off your mental turmoil:

6 easy steps to cut down tensions, unease and too much thinking

Dr Kenny P. Cook

Copyright

Table of contents

Introduction

Do your thoughts, feelings, and anxieties ever cause you to feel like you are drowning in them? Because of the emotional turbulence you're experiencing, do you ever find it difficult to concentrate, relax, or sleep? Do you ever find yourself wishing that you might gain more mental clarity and live a life that is more peaceful, clear, and joyful?

This book is perfect for you if you responded yes to any of the questions that were presented to you. Through the utilization of six simple techniques that are founded on scientific study and practical experience, this book is intended to assist you in easing the mental turbulence that you are experiencing, as well as reducing the amount of anxiety, discomfort, and excessive thinking that you endure.

It is as simple as these six steps:

1. Cognitive restructuring: How to transform your illogical, negative, or harmful thoughts, and to replace them with more reasonable, positive, or useful ones.

2. Emotional regulation: How to recognize, classify, accept, and regulate your emotions, and to select and act on them intelligently and effectively.

3. Mindfulness: Mindfulness is the practice of being present, aware, and attentive to one's experiences, as well as the ability to watch and accept such experiences without reacting or passing judgment on them.

4. Gratitude: How to recognize and show gratitude for what you have, as well as how to concentrate on the positive parts of your life, is what is referred to as gratitude.

5. Self-compassion: How to be kind, compassionate, and forgiving toward oneself, especially when you are hurting or struggling.

6. Sleep hygiene: How to increase your sleep quality and quantity, and to optimize your routines and behaviors that support excellent sleep.

In the event that you adhere to these six simple methods, you will be able to:

Mental turmoil

1. Reduce your tension, worry, and negativity, and boost your happiness, optimism, and well-being.
2. Enhance your attention, focus, and memory, and increase your cognition, learning, and performance.
3. Strengthen your connections, communication, and social skills, and strengthen your connection, support, and belonging.
4. Achieve your goals, aspirations, and potential, and boost your mental clarity and well-being.
In this book, you will find:

1. An explanation of each stage, and why it is vital and beneficial for wiping off your mental turbulence, and for cutting down your stress, discomfort, and too much pondering.
2. A discussion of the tools, strategies, and suggestions that you may use to implement each stage, and how to practice and master them.
3. A presentation of the examples, exercises, and activities that you may use to practice each stage, and how to apply them to your own problems and obstacles.

We hope that you will find this book helpful and enlightening and that you will enjoy reading it as much as we have loved creating it. We also hope that you will share your feedback, questions, and stories with us, and that you will join our community of readers and learners who are also on the same road as you. Together, we can wash off our mental anguish, and gain better mental clarity.

Part 1: Understanding Mental Turmoil

Mental upheaval is a condition of mental pain that strikes many people at some time in their lives. It might show as worry, despair, rage, guilt, shame, or

Mental turmoil

other negative feelings that interfere with one's well-being and functioning. Mental turbulence can be induced by several circumstances, such as trauma, stress, bereavement, conflict, or unfulfilled needs. It can also be impacted by one's personality, temperament, coping abilities, and social support.

Mental turbulence is not a sign of weakness or failure. It is a natural and human response to tough conditions and experiences. However, when mental turbulence becomes persistent, strong, or overpowering, it might hinder one's capacity to manage and enjoy life. It can also lead to medical, psychological, and social difficulties, such as sleeplessness, weariness, disease, low self-esteem, isolation, or drug misuse.

The good news is that mental turbulence can be resolved with the correct treatment and support. There are numerous helpful techniques to manage mental turbulence, such as therapy, medicine, self-care, relaxation, mindfulness, or positive affirmations. These tactics can enable one to reduce stress, manage emotions, resolve disputes, heal wounds, and promote well-being. By understanding the origins and repercussions of mental turbulence,

Mental turmoil

one may also acquire better compassion, empathy, and resilience.
we shall address the following issues on this part:

- What is mental unrest and how does it influence us?
- What are the common causes and triggers of mental turmoil?
- What are the indications and symptoms of mental turmoil?
- How can we cope with emotional upheaval in healthy and beneficial ways?
- How can we avoid or lessen emotional distress in the future?

Chapter 1

The Grip of Mental Turmoil: Recognizing the Symptoms and Impact

Mental anguish may impact everyone, regardless of age, gender, culture, or background. It might be a momentary or a long-term disorder, depending on the degree and length of the anguish. Mental upheaval may have a tremendous influence on one's physical, mental, and social well-being, as well as one's quality of life.

Some of the frequent signs of mental disturbance are:

Mental turmoil

Emotional symptoms: These include emotions of worry, despair, wrath, guilt, humiliation, fear, or hopelessness. One may also feel mood changes, anger, or numbness.

Cognitive symptoms: These include difficulty in thinking, focusing, remembering, or making judgments. One may also have negative or skewed ideas, such as self-criticism, blame, or pessimism.

Behavioral symptoms: These include changes in one's conduct, habits, or routines. One may also engage in undesirable or destructive habits, such as isolation, avoidance, procrastination, aggressiveness, or substance misuse.

Physical symptoms: These include changes in one's body functioning, feelings, or looks. One may also feel bodily discomfort or pain, such as headaches, stomachaches, sleeplessness, exhaustion, or weight loss or increase.

The impact of mental upheaval might vary from person to person, based on the severity, frequency, and length of the suffering, as well as the coping resources and support available. Some of the probable repercussions of mental turbulence are:

Mental turmoil

Impaired functioning: Mental turmoil might impair one's ability to complete daily duties, such as work, school, or domestic chores. It can also influence one's performance, productivity, or creativity.

Reduced well-being: Mental anguish can impair one's sense of enjoyment, satisfaction, or fulfillment. It can also affect one's self-esteem, confidence, or identity.

Damaged relationships: Mental anguish can damage one's interactions and ties with others, such as family, friends, or colleagues. It can also produce disagreements, misunderstandings, or solitude.

Increased risks: Mental instability can expose one to different dangers or damages, such as accidents, injuries, diseases, or assault. It can also raise the chance of acquiring other mental problems, such as depression, anxiety, or post-traumatic stress disorder.

Mental instability is not something to be embarrassed of or disregarded. It is a significant and prevalent condition that demands treatment and care. By identifying the signs and consequences of mental turbulence, one may take the first step towards getting treatment and support, and eventually, overcoming the pain and restoring one's well-being.

Chapter 2

The Culprits: Identifying Common Triggers and Thought Patterns

Mental anguish is not a random or accidental phenomenon. It is typically the outcome of particular events, situations, or experiences that trigger or intensify one's emotional anguish. These triggers can be external or internal, and they can vary from person to person, depending on one's sensitivity, vulnerability, and past. Some of the common triggers of mental distress are:

Mental turmoil

Trauma: Trauma is a very upsetting or disturbing experience that overwhelms one's ability to cope. It might be a single incident, such as an accident, attack, or natural disaster, or a sequence of events, like abuse, neglect, or war. Trauma can have enduring repercussions on one's physical and mental health, such as flashbacks, nightmares, anxiety, or sadness.

Stress: Stress is a state of mental or emotional strain or tension stemming from demanding or stressful situations. It might be acute, such as a deadline, exam, or interview, or persistent, such as a job, relationship, or sickness. Stress may impact one's attitude, conduct, and well-being, such as creating irritation, weariness, or sleeplessness.

Loss: Loss is the state or sensation of being deprived of something or someone that one loves or cares about. It might be concrete, such as a death, divorce, or relocation, or intangible, such as a breakup, betrayal, or rejection. Loss can induce grief, sadness, anger, or guilt, and it can also impair one's sense of identity, purpose, or belonging.

Conflict: Conflict is a condition of disagreement, antagonism, or incompatibility between two or more parties. It can be interpersonal, such as a quarrel, dispute, or misunderstanding, or intrapersonal, such as a problem, uncertainty, or remorse. Conflict may generate irritation, resentment, or animosity, and it can also destroy one's self-esteem, trust, or harmony.

Unmet needs: Unmet needs are the state or emotion of lacking something that one requires or craves for one's well-being or pleasure. They can be physical, such as food, drink, or sleep, or psychological, such as love, respect, or acknowledgment. Unmet wants can lead to unhappiness, discontent, or emptiness, and they can also push one to seek or fulfill them in unhealthy or hazardous ways.

In addition to these triggers, mental turmoil is also impacted by one's thinking patterns or the way one perceives and assesses one's events, feelings, and behaviors. Thought patterns can be reasonable or irrational, pleasant or negative, useful or harmful. Some of the prevalent thinking patterns that contribute to mental anguish are:

Catastrophizing: Catastrophizing is the propensity to envision or predict the worst possible conclusion of a situation, or to exaggerate the negative implications of an occurrence.

Overgeneralizing: Overgeneralizing is the propensity to make wide and sweeping conclusions based on a single or limited evidence, or to assign a negative label to oneself or others based on a specific feature or action. For example, I made a mistake, I am a failure, I can't do anything correctly.

Personalizing: Personalizing is the inclination to take things personally or to blame oneself for things that are not one's fault or responsibility, or to assign other people's actions or feelings to oneself. For example, He didn't call me back, he must dislike me, I must have done something wrong.

Filtering: Filtering is the propensity to focus on the bad parts of a situation or event, while disregarding or minimizing the good ones, or to accentuate one's defects or shortcomings while downplaying or rejecting one's strengths or successes.

- **All-or-nothing thinking:** All-or-nothing thinking is the propensity to perceive things in black-and-white or extreme terms, without considering the shades of gray or the middle ground, or to evaluate oneself or others based on strict or unrealistic standards or expectations. For example, I ate a slice of cake, I violated my diet, I am a loser, I might as well devour the whole cake.

These thinking patterns can distort one's perspective of reality, and they can also reinforce or worsen one's emotional suffering. By recognizing the

Mental turmoil

frequent triggers and thought patterns of mental turbulence, one may obtain a greater knowledge of the origins and effects of one's suffering, and also develop more awareness and control over one's thoughts and emotions.

Chapter 3

The Science of Serenity: Exploring the Neuroscience of Stress and Relaxation

Mental turbulence is not just a psychological issue, but also a physiological one. It includes the activation of several brain areas, hormones, and neurotransmitters that govern our stress and relaxation responses. By studying the biology of stress and relaxation, we may learn how to adjust our brain activity and chemistry, and therefore, boost our mental and emotional well-being.

Stress is a normal and adaptive response to perceived or actual dangers or challenges. It prepares us to fight or run from danger, by boosting our heart rate, blood pressure, respiration, and muscular tension. It also promotes the production of chemicals, such as adrenaline and cortisol, that boost

Mental turmoil

our alertness, energy, and focus. Stress may be useful in tiny doses since it can assist us to perform better, cope with challenges, or conquer hurdles. However, when stress becomes chronic, overwhelming, or unmanageable, it can have adverse impacts on our health and happiness. Chronic stress can affect our immune system, digestive system, cardiovascular system, and reproductive system. It can also harm our brain cells, especially in the hippocampus, the area responsible for memory and learning. Chronic stress may also affect our brain chemistry, by lowering the amounts of neurotransmitters, such as serotonin and dopamine, that govern our mood, motivation, and enjoyment.

Relaxation is the antithesis of tension. It is a condition of quiet, peace, and harmony that restores our bodily and mental equilibrium. Relaxation includes the activation of the parasympathetic nervous system, the branch of the autonomic nervous system that governs our rest and digestion processes. It decreases our heart rate, blood pressure, respiration, and muscular tension. It also increases the production of chemicals, such as oxytocin and endorphins, that boost our social connection, trust, and happiness. Relaxation may be useful in many ways since it can enable us to heal, recuperate, or revitalize.

There are several efficient strategies to produce relaxation, such as meditation, yoga, breathing exercises, massage, music, or aromatherapy. These strategies can enable us to reduce stress, quiet our thoughts, and relax our body. They can also enhance our brain function and structure, by boosting the activity and growth of the prefrontal cortex, the area responsible for executive processes, such as planning, decision-making, and self-control. They can also raise the amounts of neurotransmitters, such as serotonin and dopamine, that govern our mood, motivation, and enjoyment.

Mental instability is not inevitable or incurable. It is a dynamic and adjustable situation that depends on our brain activity and chemistry. By examining the neurology of stress and relaxation, we may obtain greater awareness and control over our mental and emotional states, and therefore, reach more peace and well-being.

Part 2: 6 Steps to Mental Clarity

Mental clarity is a desirable and attainable state of mind that may boost your well-being, productivity, and creativity. However, gaining mental clarity is not always simple, especially in today's fast-paced and hectic society. Fortunately, there are several easy and effective methods that you may use to clear your mind and improve your attention. Here are six strategies for mental clarity that you may implement in your daily life:

1. Declutter your surroundings. A crowded environment may generate a cluttered mind, since it distracts your attention, diminishes your efficiency, and raises your stress. To declutter your surroundings, you might start by arranging your workstation, house, or any other area where you spend a lot of time. You may also get rid of any unwanted or underused objects that eat up space and energy. By cleaning your surroundings, you may create a more pleasant, comfortable, and favorable atmosphere for your mental clarity.

Mental turmoil

2. Declutter your mind. A crowded mind may also hamper your mental clarity since it fills your head with irrelevant, unpleasant, or repeated ideas that interfere with your attention and recall. To clear your mind, you can start by writing down anything that is on your mind, such as your chores, objectives, anxieties, or thoughts. You may also use a notebook, a calendar, or an app to organize your ideas and prioritize your tasks. By clearing your mind, you may free up your mental space and lower your mental burden.

3. Manage your stress. Stress is one of the primary enemies of mental clarity, as it triggers your fight-or-flight reaction, which hinders your cognitive skills, such as thinking, problem-solving, and decision-making. To manage your stress, you might start by recognizing the origins and triggers of your stress and finding strategies to cope with them or avoid them. You may also utilize relaxation techniques, such as meditation, breathing exercises, or yoga, to quiet your nervous system and restore your mental equilibrium.

4. Sleep soundly. Sleep is vital for mental clarity since it enables your brain to consolidate your memories, process your emotions, and repair your cells. Sleep also modulates your hormones, such as cortisol and melatonin, which impact your mood, energy, and alertness. To sleep effectively, you may start by maintaining a regular sleep schedule, avoiding coffee, alcohol, or nicotine before bed, and setting a dark, quiet, and comfortable resting environment. You may also use a sleep tracker, a white noise machine, or an eye mask to increase your sleep quality and length.

5. Eat well. Eating correctly is also vital for mental clarity since it gives your brain the nutrition, vitamins, and minerals that it needs to function efficiently. Eating correctly also stabilizes your blood sugar levels, which impact your mood, focus, and motivation. To eat healthily, you may start by following a balanced and diverse diet, rich in fruits, vegetables, whole grains, lean meats, and healthy fats. You may also avoid processed meals, refined sugars, and artificial additives, which might harm your brain health and function.

6. Exercise frequently. Exercise is another crucial aspect of mental clarity, as it boosts your blood flow, oxygen, and glucose to your brain, which enhances your cognitive functions, such as memory, attention, and creativity. Exercise also produces endorphins, serotonin, and dopamine, which increase your mood, confidence, and contentment.

Mental turmoil

To exercise frequently, you can start by selecting a physical activity that you love, such as walking, jogging, cycling, or dancing. You may also create reasonable and detailed goals, measure your progress, and reward yourself for your successes.

By following these six steps, you may increase your mental clarity and experience the advantages of a clear and focused mind. Mental clarity is not a set or permanent condition, but a dynamic and adaptable one, that demands your ongoing attention and care. However, with little effort and dedication, you can make mental clarity a habit and a lifestyle that will benefit your personal and professional progress.

Chapter 4

Breathe Away the Tension: Mastering Mindfulness and Breathwork

One of the most effective and accessible instruments for mental clarity is your own breath. Breathing is not just a crucial function that supports your existence, but also a portal to your thoughts and emotions. By learning how to breathe deliberately and intentionally, you can impact your mental and emotional states, and gain increased tranquility, attention, and awareness.

Here we will speak about two disciplines that include the use of breath: mindfulness and breathwork. Mindfulness is the discipline of paying attention to the present moment, with openness, curiosity, and acceptance. Breathwork is the practice of employing various breathing methods to achieve certain purposes, such as relaxation, energization, or healing. Both techniques can assist you to clear your mind, lower your tension, and boost your well-being.

Mindfulness: The Art of Being Present

Mindfulness is a simple yet powerful practice that may alter your life. Mindfulness is the ability to be fully present in the here and now, without being distracted by the past or the future, or by judgments, expectations, or views. Mindfulness is also the capacity to notice your thoughts, feelings, sensations, and impulses, without responding to them or identifying with them. Mindfulness is a skill that can be fostered by regular practice, and it may provide numerous advantages to your mental and emotional health, such as:

Increased awareness: Mindfulness may enable you to become more aware of yourself and your environment, and to notice the fine details and subtleties that you may otherwise overlook. Mindfulness may also enable you to become more aware of your habits, patterns, and triggers, and to notice when you are operating on autopilot or out of sync with your values and aspirations.

Improved focus: Mindfulness can assist you to enhance your concentration and attention span, and to filter out the noise and distractions that might muddle your mind. Mindfulness can also assist you to enhance your memory and recall and to retain and absorb information more efficiently.

Reduced stress: Mindfulness can assist you in reducing your stress levels and coping with stressors more calmly and logically. Mindfulness can also assist you in reducing your blood pressure, heart rate, and cortisol levels, and activate your parasympathetic nervous system, which is responsible for your rest and digestion functions.

Enhanced mood: Mindfulness can assist you to boost your mood and to control your emotions more successfully. Mindfulness can also assist you in raising your levels of serotonin and dopamine, which are neurotransmitters that impact your happiness and motivation. Mindfulness can also enable you to create good feelings, such as appreciation, pleasure, and compassion.

Greater well-being: Mindfulness can assist you to enhance your general well-being and quality of life, by raising your self-esteem, self-compassion, and self-acceptance. Mindfulness may also assist you to strengthen your relationships, by enhancing your empathy, communication, and closeness. Mindfulness may also enable you to find more meaning and purpose in your life, by connecting your actions with your beliefs and interests.

How to Practice Mindfulness

There are various ways to practice mindfulness, and you may select the ones that suit your interests, requirements, and objectives. However, the underlying principles of mindfulness remain the same, regardless of the approach or methodology. Here are some broad recommendations on how to practice mindfulness:

Set aside some time and space: To practice mindfulness, you need to allocate some time and space for yourself, where you may be free from interruptions and distractions. You can start with a few minutes a day, and gradually increase the time and frequency of your practice. You can also find a comfortable and peaceful spot, where you can sit, stand, or lie down, depending on the sort of exercise you are performing.

Mental turmoil

Choose a focus: To practice mindfulness, you need to choose a focus for your attention, such as your breath, your body, your senses, your thoughts, your feelings, or an item. You can also pick a specific subject or topic, such as gratitude, kindness, or forgiveness. The focus of your attention can enable you to anchor your mind in the current moment and prevent it from straying or drifting.

notice and accept: To cultivate mindfulness, you need to notice and accept whatever emerges in your consciousness, without judging, analyzing, or opposing it. You can employ a compassionate and interesting approach, and treat your experience as if you are experiencing it for the first time. You may also utilize a loving and forgiving mindset, and treat yourself and others as if you are your greatest friend. The goal is to be open and receptive to whatever is happening in the here and now and to let go of any attachment or aversion to it.

Return and repeat: To practice mindfulness, you need to return and repeat the process of focusing, observing, and accepting, whenever your mind wanders or becomes distracted. You can use a kind and pleasant reminder, such as a word, a phrase, or a gesture, to return your attention back to your focus. You may also use a soft and friendly recognition, such as a smile, a nod, or a thank you, to recognize your effort and development. The goal is to be patient and persistent and to know that mindfulness is a practice, not a destination.

Some Examples of Mindfulness Practices

Here are some examples of mindfulness techniques that you may attempt, based on your tastes, requirements, and goals:

Mindful breathing: Mindful breathing is the discipline of paying attention to your breath, as it flows in and out of your body. You may watch the feelings, emotions, and noises of your breath, and see how it influences your mind and body. You may also utilize your breath as a technique to relax your nervous system, by inhaling deeply, slowly, and evenly. You may practice mindful breathing anytime and anywhere, and use it as a technique to center yourself and relax.

Mindful body scan: Mindful body scan is the discipline of paying attention to your body, as it rests or moves. You can scan your body from head to toe, or from toe to head, and observe any sensations, feelings, or emotions that occur in each section of your body. You may also utilize your body as a tool to alleviate any tension, pain, or discomfort, by inhaling into the afflicted areas and then relaxing them with your exhale. You may practice mindful body scans as a technique to connect with your body and to promote your physical health and well-being.

Mindful eating: Mindful eating is the discipline of paying attention to your food, while you prepare, serve, and enjoy it. You may study the colors, forms, textures, scents, and tastes of your meal, and note how it impacts your senses, hunger, and pleasure. You may also utilize your food as a tool to nurture your body, mind, and soul, by choosing nutritious and tasty meals and eating them with appreciation and satisfaction. You may practice mindful eating as a technique to enhance your eating habits and to appreciate your food and its suppliers.

Mindful walking: Mindful walking is the technique of paying attention to your walking, as you move through your environment. You may watch the feelings, motions, and rhythms of your feet, legs, and body, and note how they interact with the ground, the air, and the gravity. You may also use your walking as a tool to explore your environment, by observing the sights, sounds, scents, and sensations that you experience along the journey. You may practice mindful walking as a means to exercise your body and discover new ideas and viewpoints.

Mindful listening: Mindful listening is the technique of paying attention to the sounds, as they reach your ears and your thoughts. You may study the loudness, pitch, tone, and quality of the sounds, and notice how they impact your mood, thoughts, and emotions. You may also utilize the sounds as a tool to interact and connect with people, by listening to their words, voices, and messages, and reacting with empathy and respect. You may practice attentive listening as a strategy to strengthen your hearing and improve your relationships.

Breathwork: The Science of Breathing

Breathwork is another exercise that incorporates the use of breath, but with a different goal and method. Breathwork is the practice of employing various breathing methods to achieve certain purposes, such as relaxation, energization, or healing. Breathwork is founded on the notion that breathing is not just a passive and automatic function, but also an active and deliberate one, that can be controlled and managed to impact our physiology, psychology, and spirituality. Breathwork may have several advantages for our health and well-being, such as:

Regulating our nervous system: Breathwork can enable us to control our nervous system, by stimulating either our sympathetic or our parasympathetic branch, depending on the kind and rate of our breathing. For example, breathing fast and shallow can trigger our sympathetic nervous system, which is responsible for our fight-or-flight response, and boosts our arousal, alertness, and energy. On the other side, breathing slowly and deeply can boost our parasympathetic nervous system, which is responsible for our rest and digestion processes, and lessen our stress, worry, and tension.

Balancing out pH levels: Breathwork can enable us to balance our pH levels, by modifying the quantity of carbon dioxide and oxygen in our blood, based on the length and ratio of our inhalation and exhale. For example, inhaling more and exhaling less can reduce the quantity of carbon dioxide raise the amount of oxygen in our blood, and make it more alkaline. On the other side, breathing less and exhaling more can boost the quantity of carbon dioxide and reduce the amount of oxygen in our blood, making it more acidic.

Chapter 5

Tame the Thought Storm: Cognitive Restructuring and Reframing Techniques

One of the biggest sources of mental stress is our own thoughts. Thoughts are the mental representations of our observations, interpretations, and judgments of ourselves, others, and the environment. Thoughts are not facts, but rather subjective and prejudiced judgments that may be impacted by different circumstances, such as our emotions, memory, experience, or culture. Thoughts may also have a tremendous influence on our emotions, habits, and well-being since they can shape our reality and our identity.

Mental turmoil

However, not all thoughts are beneficial or correct. Some ideas are illogical, unpleasant, or unhelpful, and they may drive us to feel and act in ways that are destructive to our health and happiness. For example, some ideas may make us feel nervous, depressed, angry, or guilty, and they can also make us behave in ways that are self-defeating, avoidant, or violent. These beliefs can also create a vicious cycle since they can reinforce and exacerbate our emotional suffering, and hinder us from recognizing or finding answers.

Fortunately, there are methods to disrupt this pattern and to calm the thought storm that may cloud our heads and hamper our mental clarity. One of the most successful strategies is to employ cognitive restructuring and reframing techniques, which are based on the principles of cognitive behavioral therapy (CBT). CBT is a style of psychotherapy that tries to transform our thoughts, attitudes, and actions, by recognizing and questioning the illogical, negative, or unhelpful beliefs that underlie them, and by replacing them with more reasonable, positive, or helpful ones. CBT can assist us to enhance our mental and emotional health, by strengthening our self-awareness, self-control, and self-efficacy.

These Are some of the approaches that will assist us in accomplishing so:

Identifying cognitive distortions: Cognitive distortions are the flaws or biases in our thinking that make us view or understand things in a skewed or erroneous way. There are various forms of cognitive distortions, such as catastrophizing, overgeneralizing, personalizing, filtering, or all-or-nothing thinking, which we have examined in Chapter 2. Identifying cognitive distortions can enable us to notice the illogical, negative, or unhelpful concepts that drive us to feel and act in undesired ways, and to dispute their validity and usefulness.

Challenging cognitive distortions: Challenging cognitive distortions is the process of challenging, testing, or arguing the erroneous, negative, or harmful views that we have discovered, and of discovering facts or arguments that contradict or weaken them. Challenging cognitive distortions can enable us to minimize the force and effect of these views and to perceive things more realistically and objectively. Challenging cognitive distortions can also enable us to build more critical and logical thinking abilities and avoid leaping to conclusions or forming assumptions.

Replacing cognitive distortions: Replacing cognitive distortions is the process of exchanging the irrational, negative, or harmful concepts that we have questioned, with more reasonable, positive, or helpful ones, that are more accurate, balanced, and constructive. Replacing cognitive distortions can assist us to modify our viewpoint and attitude, and to feel and act in more productive and adaptive ways. Replacing cognitive distortions can also assist us to create more positive and resilient thinking patterns, and to cope with difficulties or obstacles more successfully.

Reframing circumstances: Reframing situations is the process of modifying the way we perceive or understand a situation, event, or experience, by finding a different or alternative meaning, purpose, or value in it. Reframing situations can assist us to recognize the positive or useful elements of a situation, or to perceive the chances or possibilities that a situation presents, rather than concentrating on the negative or detrimental ones. Reframing situations may also assist us in discovering more motivation and inspiration and reaching more pleasure and fulfillment.

How to Use Cognitive Restructuring and Reframing Techniques

There are various methods to apply cognitive restructuring and reframing strategies, and you may select the ones that suit your tastes, requirements, and goals. However, the core stages of employing these strategies remain the same, regardless of the method or instrument. Here are some broad tips on how to employ cognitive restructuring and reframing techniques:

Identify the scenario: To apply cognitive restructuring and reframing strategies, you need to identify the circumstance, event, or experience that is giving you mental anguish, and that you wish to modify or better. You may also identify the feelings, actions, and outcomes that are related to the scenario, and how they influence your well-being and functioning.

Identify the ideas: To apply cognitive restructuring and reframing strategies, you need to identify the thoughts that are relevant to the circumstance, and that are impacting your emotions and behaviors. You can use a thought record, a notebook, or an app to jot down your thoughts and evaluate them in terms of their content, frequency, and intensity. You may also use a rating scale, to quantify how much you believe or feel each notion.

recognize the distortions: To apply cognitive restructuring and reframing strategies, you need to recognize the cognitive distortions that are present in your thinking, and that are making them unreasonable, unpleasant, or unhelpful. You can use a list, a chart, or a worksheet to compare your ideas with the typical forms of cognitive distortions and to classify them properly. You may also use a rating system, to determine how much each distortion influences your ideas.

confront the distortions: To apply cognitive restructuring and reframing strategies, you need to confront the cognitive distortions that you have discovered and uncover facts or arguments that contradict or weaken them. You can use a series of questions, such as, Is this thought true?Is this thinking helpful?, What is the evidence for or against this thought?, or What is another way to look at this situation?, to investigate and assess your views. You may also use a rating scale, to quantify how much your belief or feeling in each notion changes after confronting it.

Replace the distortions: To apply cognitive restructuring and reframing strategies, you need to replace the cognitive distortions that you have questioned, with more reasonable, positive, or helpful beliefs that are more accurate, balanced, and useful. You can use a statement, a phrase, or a mantra, to convey your new views, and to affirm them to yourself. You may also use a rating scale, to quantify how much your belief or emotion in each notion changes after changing it.

Reframe the scenario: To employ cognitive restructuring and reframing strategies, you need to reframe the situation that you have recognized and discover a different or alternative meaning, purpose, or value in it. You can utilize a question, such as "What can I learn from this scenario?", "What would I do differently in this situation?, or "How would I make the best of this situation?, to investigate and uncover new ways to perceive or interpret the event. You may also use a grading system, to quantify how much your viewpoint and attitude change after reframing the scenario.

Some Examples of Cognitive Restructuring and Reframing Techniques

Here are some examples of cognitive restructuring and reframing approaches that you may use, based on your preferences, requirements, and goals:

The ABCDE model. The ABCDE model is a cognitive restructuring strategy that employs the acronym ABCDE to help you through the process of discovering and modifying your ideas. The ABCDE stands for:

A: Activating event. This is the scenario, event, or experience that prompts your thoughts, feelings, and behaviors.

B: Beliefs. These are the ideas that you have regarding the activating event, and that impact your moods and behaviors.

C: Consequences. These are the sensations and behaviors that come from your beliefs, and that impact your well-being and functioning.

D: Disputation. This is the process of testing your views and discovering facts or arguments that contradict or undermine them.

Mental turmoil

E: Effect. This is the conclusion of the disputation and the changes that occur in your views, feelings, and behaviors.

For example, assume you have a presentation at work, and you are feeling apprehensive and tense. You may utilize the ABCDE model as follows:

A: Activating event. The presentation at work.
B: Beliefs. I am not excellent at public speaking. I will botch up and disgrace myself. Everyone will think I am inept and foolish.
C: Consequences. You feel worried, tense, and insecure. You avoid planning or practicing for the presentation. You perform poorly and make blunders during the presentation.
D: Disputation. "Is this thought true? No, I have done presentations before, and I have received positive feedback and compliments. Is this thought helpful? No, it makes me feel worse and prevents me from doing my best. What is the evidence of this thought? There is no evidence that I am not good at public speaking, or that I will mess up and embarrass myself. There is no evidence that everyone will think I am incompetent and stupid.

Mental turmoil

This is an opportunity to showcase my skills and knowledge and to impress my boss and colleagues. I can prepare and practice well, and deliver a confident and successful presentation.

E: Effect. You feel more calm, confident, and prepared. You practice and rehearse your presentation. You perform well and win acclaim and accolades from your audience.

F: Feedback. This is the process of analyzing the influence of the disputation and reinforcing the changes that happened in your views, feelings, and behaviors. You may also utilize this phase to highlight any areas for improvement or additional action.

For example, you may utilize the feedback as follows:

F: Feedback. It made me feel more calm, confident and prepared. It made me practice and rehearse my presentation. It made me perform well and receive applause and praise from my audience. What did I learn from this experience? I learned that I can challenge and change my irrational, negative, or unhelpful thoughts and that doing so can improve my mental and emotional health, and my performance and outcomes. What can I do to maintain or enhance these changes? I can continue to use the ABCDE model whenever I face a similar situation or any other situation that causes me mental turmoil. I can also practice and improve my public speaking skills, and seek more opportunities to present and share my work.

The ABCDE model is a simple and effective cognitive restructuring strategy that you may use to control your thought storm and attain better mental clarity. You may use it to deal with any scenario, event, or experience that stimulates your illogical, negative, or unhelpful ideas, and to replace them with more reasonable, positive, or helpful ones.

The 3Cs model: The 3Cs model is a reframing strategy that employs the acronym 3Cs to lead you through the process of altering your viewpoint and attitude. The 3Cs stand for:

Challenge: This is the process of challenging or testing your existing perspective or attitude, and finding out if it is correct, practical, or constructive. You can utilize a series of questions, such as "Is this viewpoint or attitude true?", "Is this perspective or attitude helpful?", or "What are the pros and disadvantages of this perspective or attitude?", to investigate and assess your perspective or attitude.

Choice: This is the process of choosing a new or alternate perspective or attitude, that is more accurate, realistic, or useful. You can utilize a series of questions, such as "What is another way to look at this scenario?", "What is a more positive or optimistic viewpoint or attitude?", or "What is a more empowering or inspirational perspective or attitude?", to examine and uncover alternative ways to see or interpret the situation.

Change: This is the process of adopting and using the new perspective or attitude, and observing the changes that occur in your emotions, behaviors, and outcomes. You can use a series of questions, such as "How does this perspective or attitude make me feel?", "How does this perspective or attitude make me act?", or "How does this perspective or attitude affect my results?", to monitor and measure the changes that occur in your emotions, behaviors, and outcomes.

For example, assume you have a challenging assignment or project to do, and you are feeling overwhelmed and disheartened. You may utilize the 3Cs model as follows:

Challenge: Is this perspective or attitude true? No, this task or project is not impossible or hopeless. It is challenging, but not insurmountable. Is this perspective or attitude helpful? No, this perspective or attitude makes me feel worse and prevents me from doing my best. What are the advantages and disadvantages of this perspective or attitude? The advantages are that it lowers my expectations and protects me from disappointment. The disadvantages are that it lowers my motivation and confidence, and increases my stress and anxiety.

Choice: This is an opportunity to learn new skills, to overcome obstacles, and to achieve something meaningful. What is a more positive or optimistic perspective or attitude? This task or project is difficult, but not impossible. It is challenging but also rewarding. What is a more empowering or inspiring perspective or attitude? I can do this task or project if I put my mind and heart into it. I have the resources, the abilities, and the support that I need to succeed.

Change: How does this attitude make me feel? It makes me feel more hopeful, excited, and proud.

Mental turmoil

How does this perspective or attitude make me act? It makes me act more proactively, creatively, and persistently. How does this perspective or attitude affect my results? It improves my results, as I complete the task or project with more quality, efficiency, and satisfaction.

The 3Cs model is a simple and powerful reframing strategy that you may use to control your thought storm and attain better mental clarity. You may use it to deal with any scenario, event, or experience that challenges your viewpoint or attitude, and to alter it to a more positive, hopeful, or empowered one.

These are some of the cognitive restructurings and reframing approaches that you might employ to control your thought storm and obtain better mental clarity. By adopting these approaches, you may transform the way you think, feel, and act, and enhance your mental and emotional health and well-being. You can also acquire greater cognitive flexibility and adaptability, and cope with obstacles or challenges more successfully.

Chapter 6

Move Your Way to Peace: Exercise and Physical Activity for Mental Well-being

One of the most effective and pleasurable methods to improve mental clarity is to move your body. Exercise and physical exercise are not only important for your physical health, but also for your mental and emotional wellbeing. By indulging in exercise and physical activity, you may clear your mind, lower your tension, and boost your well-being.

Let's speak about the advantages of exercise and physical activity for mental well-being, and the types and intensities of exercise and physical activity that are suited and good for different objectives and needs. We will also share some recommendations and suggestions on how to start, continue, and enjoy exercise and physical activity, and how to overcome some of the usual hurdles and problems that may hinder or discourage you from moving your body.

The Benefits of Exercise and Physical Activity for Mental Well-being

Exercise and physical exercise can have various advantages for your mental and emotional health, such as:

Improving your mood: Exercise and physical exercise can assist you to enhance your mood and to control your emotions more successfully. Exercise and physical exercise can boost the production of endorphins, serotonin, and dopamine, which are neurotransmitters that alter your happiness, motivation, and enjoyment. Exercise and physical activity can help lower the levels of cortisol and adrenaline, which are chemicals that impact your stress, anxiety, and tension.

Mental turmoil

Boosting your energy: Exercise and physical activity can assist you in raising your energy and overcoming exhaustion and lethargy. Exercise and physical exercise can boost your blood flow, oxygen, and glucose to your brain and body, which enhances your cognitive and physical capacities. Exercise and physical activity can also enhance your sleep quality and length, which impact your mood, concentration, and alertness.

Enhancing your self-esteem: Exercise and physical exercise may assist you to boost your self-esteem and to feel more confident and proud of yourself. Exercise and physical exercise may enhance your physical appearance, health, and fitness, which can make you feel more attractive, healthy, and fit. Exercise and physical exercise may also boost your performance, productivity, and creativity, which can make you feel more competent, successful, and happy.

Strengthening your connections: Exercise and physical activity can enable you to build your relationships and to connect with people more deeply and profoundly. Exercise and physical exercise can give the opportunity to meet new people, share mutual interests, and support and encourage each other. Exercise and physical activity can also boost the production of oxytocin, which is a hormone that impacts your social connection, trust, and intimacy.

Finding more meaning and purpose: Exercise and physical exercise may assist you to find more meaning and purpose in your life, by connecting your activities with your values and passions. Exercise and physical exercise may offer a feeling of direction, motivation, and inspiration, and can enable you to attain your goals and objectives. Exercise and physical exercise may also bring a sense of pleasure, happiness, and thankfulness, and can enable you to appreciate your life and its origins.

The Types and Levels of Exercise and Physical Activity

There are different sorts and levels of exercise and physical activity, and you may select the ones that suit your tastes, requirements, and goals. However, the basic categories of exercise and physical activity are:

Aerobic activity: Aerobic exercise is the form of exercise that involves continuous and rhythmic motions of major muscle groups, such as walking, jogging, cycling, or swimming. Aerobic exercise can enhance your cardiovascular health, by strengthening your heart, lungs, and blood vessels. Aerobic exercise can also enhance your endurance, by boosting your capacity to maintain physical activity for extended periods of time.

Anaerobic exercise: Anaerobic exercise is the form of exercise that involves brief and intense bursts of activity, such as running, leaping, or lifting weights. Anaerobic exercise can enhance your muscular health, by strengthening your muscles, bones, and joints. Anaerobic exercise can also boost your power, by enhancing your capacity to create force and speed in a short amount of time.

Flexibility exercise: Flexibility exercise is a form of exercise that involves stretching and extending your muscles, tendons, and ligaments, such as yoga, pilates, or tai chi. Flexibility training can increase your mobility, by improving your range of motion and lowering your stiffness and soreness. Flexibility training can help enhance your balance, by boosting your stability and coordination.

Mind-body exercise: Mind-body exercise is a form of exercise that involves connecting your mind and body, by using your breath, consciousness, and intention, such as meditation, breathing exercises, or mindfulness. Mind-body exercise may enhance your mental health, by relaxing your mind, lowering your tension, and boosting your well-being. Mind-body exercise may also enhance your emotional health, by controlling your emotions, boosting your empathy, and nurturing your compassion.

The amounts of exercise and physical activity might vary from person to person, depending on their age, health, fitness, and aspirations. However, the basic standards for the amounts of exercise and physical activity are:

Frequency: Frequency is how often you exercise or engage in physical activity. The suggested frequency for most adults is at least three times a week, for at least 20 minutes each time. However, you may vary the frequency according to your schedule, tastes, and needs.

Intensity: Intensity is how hard you work or engage in physical activity. The suggested level for most individuals is moderate to vigorous, which means that you should feel your heart rate and respiration increase, but not to the point where you cannot talk or feel uncomfortable. However, you may alter the intensity according to your talents, tastes, and needs.

Duration: Duration is how long you work or engage in physical activity. The suggested length for most individuals is at least 150 minutes of moderate effort 75 minutes of vigorous intensity each week, or a mix of both. However, you may change the time according to your goals, interests, and needs.

How to Start, Maintain, and Enjoy Exercise and Physical Activity

Starting, continuing, and enjoying exercise and physical activity can be tough for some people, especially if they have physical, mental, or emotional hurdles or problems that restrict or discourage them from moving their bodies. However, there are certain advice and recommendations that may enable you to overcome these hurdles and problems and to make exercise and physical activity a part of your life. Here are some recommendations and suggestions on how to start, maintain, and enjoy exercise and physical activity:

Mental turmoil

Start slowly and gradually: To start exercise and physical activity, you do not need to do too much or too fast. You may start with tiny and progressive measures, such as walking for 10 minutes a day or completing some stretches in the morning. You may also increase the frequency, intensity, and length of your exercise and physical activity gradually, as you feel more comfortable and confident. By starting softly and gradually, you can prevent injury, burnout, or frustration, and you can also build your habit and momentum.

find something you love: To sustain and enjoy exercise and physical activity, you need to find something that you enjoy and that meets your personality, interests, and goals. You may experiment with numerous sorts and amounts of exercise and physical activity, and find the ones that make you feel good, happy, and content. You may also change your workout and physical activity, and attempt new activities, to keep yourself motivated and engaged.

create realistic and precise objectives: To continue and enjoy exercise and physical activity, you need to create realistic and defined goals that are attainable and quantifiable. You can utilize the SMART criterion, which stands for Specific,

Measurable, Achievable, Relevant, and Time-bound, to define your objectives. By creating realistic and detailed objectives, you can measure your progress, celebrate your victories, and reward yourself for your efforts.

Find a companion or a group: To sustain and enjoy exercise and physical activity, you may find a partner or a group that can support and encourage you, and that can share your experience and delight. You can discover a partner or a group that has comparable or complementary objectives, tastes, and requirements, and that can give you feedback, guidance, or companionship. You may also join a class, a club, or an online community that can provide you with assistance, teaching, or inspiration. By finding a partner or a group, you may improve your accountability, dedication, and pleasure.

Be flexible and adaptable: To continue and enjoy exercise and physical activity, you need to be flexible and adaptable and to alter your exercise and physical activity according to your circumstances, conditions, and demands. You may be flexible and adaptive by having a backup plan, such as conducting indoor workouts when the weather is terrible, or completing shorter activities when you are busy. You may also be flexible and adaptable by

Mental turmoil

listening to your body and respecting your boundaries, such as taking a break when you are fatigued, or altering your activities when you are wounded. By being flexible and adaptive, you can prevent or overcome challenges, and you can also prevent or lessen boredom, worry, or guilt.

Chapter 7

Nurture Your Calm: Cultivating Gratitude, Self-Compassion, and Positive Habits

Achieving mental clarity is not just a question of changing your ideas, feelings, and actions, but also of fostering your calm, which is the condition of being peaceful, serene, and content. Nurturing your calm may enable you to minimize your stress, anxiety, and negativity, and to boost your happiness, optimism, and well-being.

These are three techniques that might help you cultivate your calm: gratitude, self-compassion, and good habits. Gratitude is the habit of being thankful and appreciative of what you have and what you experience. Self-compassion is the discipline of being compassionate and understanding toward yourself, especially when you are hurting or struggling. Positive habits are the behaviors that you perform frequently and consistently that promote your physical, mental, and emotional health and well-being.

Gratitude: The Power of Appreciation

Gratitude is a simple yet powerful discipline that may alter your life. Gratitude is the capacity to identify and acknowledge the positive things that you have and that you experience, such as your health, your family, your friends, your successes, or your possibilities. Gratitude is also the capacity to communicate and convey your gratitude and thankfulness, either orally, in writing, or in action. Gratitude is a talent that can be acquired by frequent practice, and it may provide various advantages to your mental and emotional health, such as:

Increasing your happiness: Gratitude can enable you to enhance your happiness and control your mood more efficiently. Gratitude may change your emphasis from what you lack or what you desire, to what you have or what you enjoy, and so, boost your contentment and fulfillment. Gratitude can also enhance your levels of serotonin and dopamine, which are neurotransmitters that impact your mood and motivation.

Reducing your stress: Gratitude can enable you to lessen your tension and to cope with stressors more calmly and logically. Gratitude can reduce your blood pressure, heart rate, and cortisol levels, and activate your parasympathetic nervous system, which is responsible for your rest and digestion processes. Gratitude may also assist you to notice the good or useful aspects of a difficult situation, or to appreciate the chances or possibilities that a stressful situation presents, rather than focusing on the negative or harmful ones.

Enhancing your connections: Gratitude may enable you to strengthen your relationships and to connect with people more deeply and profoundly. Gratitude may give opportunities to express and receive gratitude, praise, and acknowledgment, and to deepen your friendships and trust. Gratitude can also boost the production of oxytocin, which is a hormone that influences your social connection, trust, and intimacy.

Improving your health: Gratitude may enable you to enhance your overall health and quality of life, by boosting your self-care, self-compassion, and self-acceptance. Gratitude may drive you to take care of your body, mind, and soul, by selecting healthy and beneficial activities, such as eating properly, sleeping well, exercising frequently, or meditating every day. Gratitude may also enable you to heal your wounds, by forgiving yourself and others, and by letting go of resentment, wrath, or guilt.

How to Practice Gratitude

There are various ways to practice thankfulness, and you may select the ones that suit your interests, requirements, and goals. However, the underlying concepts of appreciation are the same, regardless of the approach or methodology. Here are some broad recommendations on how to cultivate gratitude:

Set aside some time and space: To practice appreciation, you need to allocate some time and space for yourself, where you may be free from interruptions and distractions. You can start with a few minutes a day, and gradually increase the time and frequency of your practice. You can also find a comfortable and peaceful spot, where you can sit, stand, or lie down, depending on the sort of exercise you are performing.

Choose a focus: To practice gratitude, you need to choose a focus for your appreciation and thankfulness, such as your health, your family, your friends, your successes, or your possibilities. You can also pick a specific subject or topic, such as your physique, your senses, your abilities, or your hobbies. The concentration of your thankfulness can enable you to anchor your attention in the present moment and prevent it from straying or drifting.

Observe and express: To practice gratitude, you need to observe and express whatever emerges in your consciousness, something you are glad for, without judging, analyzing, or opposing it. You can employ a compassionate and interesting approach, and treat your experience as if you are experiencing it for the first time. You may also employ a loving and giving mindset, and treat yourself and others as if you are your closest friend. The goal is to be open and sensitive to whatever is happening in the here and now and to express and share your appreciation and thankfulness, either orally, in writing, or in action.

Return and repeat: To practice appreciation, you need to return and repeat the process of focusing, observing, and expressing, whenever your mind wanders or becomes distracted. You can use a kind and pleasant reminder, such as a word, a phrase, or a gesture, to return your attention back to your focus. You may also use a soft and friendly recognition, such as a smile, a nod, or a thank you, to recognize your effort and development. The key is to be patient and persistent and to know that thankfulness is a practice, not a destination.

Some Examples of Gratitude Practices

Here are some examples of thankfulness practices that you can attempt, based on your interests, needs, and goals:

Gratitude diary: A gratitude journal is the habit of writing down the things that you are grateful for, on a daily or weekly basis. You can write down everything that you are grateful for, large or small, such as your health, your family, your friends, your successes, or your prospects. You may also write down why you are grateful for them, and how they make you feel. You may use a notebook, a planner, or an app to keep your thankfulness diary, and you can review it periodically, to remind yourself of the positive things in your life.

Gratitude letter: A gratitude letter is the practice of writing a letter to someone who has made a good influence in your life, and expressing your appreciation and thankfulness for them. You can write a letter to anybody who has helped, supported, or inspired you, such as your family, your friends, your instructors, your mentors, or your heroes. You may also write a letter to yourself, and express your gratitude and admiration for your own characteristics, abilities, and successes. You can either mail or deliver the letter to the recipient or retain it for yourself, based on your desire and comfort.

Gratitude meditation: A gratitude meditation is the practice of concentrating on the things that you are grateful for, and feeling the emotions that they trigger in you. You can meditate on anything that you are grateful for, such as your breath, your body, your senses, your abilities, or your hobbies. You can also focus on the individuals who have made a good influence in your life, and experience the love, joy, and tranquility that they provide to you. You may use a guided meditation, a mantra, or music, to help you focus and relax, and you can also make a gesture, such as resting your palm over your heart, to increase your connection and expression.

Gratitude walk: A gratitude walk is the practice of going through your environment, identifying the things that you are glad for, and expressing your appreciation and thankfulness for them. You can stroll around any location, such as your neighborhood, your park, or your city, and note the sights, sounds, scents, and sensations that you experience along the route. You may also show your appreciation and thanks, either orally, in writing, or in action, such as saying thank you, writing a note, or presenting a gift, to the people, places, or things that you are grateful for.

Gratitude is a simple and effective technique that you may use to cultivate inner calm and to obtain increased mental clarity. You may utilize it to appreciate and enjoy the wonderful things in your life, and to manage the hardships or obstacles that you confront. You may also utilize it to promote more good feelings, such as happiness, optimism, and well-being.

Self-Compassion: The Power of Kindness

Self-compassion is another easy yet effective practice that may alter your life. Self-compassion is the ability to be compassionate and understanding toward yourself, especially when you are hurting or struggling. Self-compassion is also the capacity to treat yourself as you would treat a friend, with care, support, and encouragement. Self-compassion is a skill that can be acquired by frequent practice, and it may provide numerous advantages to your mental and emotional health, such as:

Reducing your pain: Self-compassion can enable you to minimize your suffering and to manage pain more efficiently. Self-compassion can allow you to notice and embrace your sorrow, without rejecting, ignoring, or concealing it. Self-compassion may also enable you to calm and relieve your discomfort, by utilizing soft and loving words, gestures, or actions. Self-compassion may also enable you to heal your suffering, by finding meaning, purpose, or worth in your misery, or by using your pain as a source of development, learning, or change.

Increasing your resilience: Self-compassion can enable you to enhance your resilience and bounce back from difficulties or obstacles more quickly and effortlessly.

Chapter 8

Sleep Your Worries Away: Optimizing Sleep Hygiene for Rest and Rejuvenation

One of the most vital and frequently disregarded parts of obtaining mental clarity is sleep. Sleep is not just a time to relax and rejuvenate, but also a time to process and consolidate your memories, emotions, and learning. Sleep is also a time to balance your hormones, such as cortisol and melatonin, which impact your mood, energy, and alertness. Sleep is an essential function that preserves your physical, mental, and emotional health and well-being.

Mental turmoil

However, many people struggle with getting enough or quality sleep, due to different causes, such as stress, anxiety, lifestyle, or environment. Lack of sleep or inadequate sleep can have harmful impacts on your mental and emotional health, such as:

Impairing your cognition: Lack of sleep or inadequate sleep can affect your cognitive processes, such as attention, concentration, memory, reasoning, problem-solving, and decision-making. Lack of sleep or bad sleep can also hamper your creativity, productivity, and performance, and increase your blunders and mistakes.

Affecting your mood: Lack of sleep or bad sleep can influence your mood and your emotional regulation, and make you more prone to unpleasant feelings, such as irritation, annoyance, rage, or melancholy. Lack of sleep or poor sleep might also make you more sensitive to mood problems, such as sadness or anxiety.

Reducing your resilience: Lack of sleep or bad sleep can diminish your resilience and your capacity to cope with difficulties or challenges and make you more sensitive to stress, burnout, or tiredness. Lack of sleep or poor sleep can also damage your immune system and your physical health, and make you more prone to diseases or infections.

Fortunately, there are strategies to increase your sleep quality and quantity, and to maximize your sleep hygiene, which is the collection of behaviors and practices that support excellent sleep. In this chapter, we will explore some of the sleep hygiene strategies and recommendations that you may use to sleep your troubles away and obtain better mental clarity. These recommendations and ideas are:

Follow a regular sleep schedule: Following a regular sleep routine can assist you to create and maintain a healthy sleep rhythm, and to synchronize your internal clock with the external light-dark cycle. Following a regular sleep pattern can also enable you to fall asleep faster, remain asleep longer, and wake up more refreshed. To follow a regular sleep pattern, you need to:

- Set a definite sleep and wake-up hour, and keep to them as much as possible, especially on weekends or holidays. You may use an alarm clock, a reminder, or an app to help you keep track of your sleep routine and to alter it gradually if required.

Mental turmoil

- Aim for at least seven to nine hours of sleep every night, which is the recommended amount for most adults, according to the National Sleep Foundation. However, you may vary the quantity according to your specific needs, tastes, and objectives.
- Avoid sleeping throughout the day, especially in the late afternoon or evening, since it might interfere with your sleep pattern and your sleep quality. However, if you feel particularly drowsy or fatigued, you can take a brief nap, of no more than 20 minutes, in the early afternoon, and at least six hours before your bedtime.

Create a pleasant and conducive sleeping environment: Creating a comfortable and favorable resting environment may assist you to relax and unwind, and to prepare your body and mind for sleep. Creating a pleasant and favorable sleeping environment can also enable you to prevent or reduce the external influences that might disrupt or disturb your sleep, such as noise, light, or temperature. To establish a pleasant and favorable resting environment, you need to:

Mental turmoil

- Make your bedroom dark, quiet, and cold, by using curtains, blinds, or shades to block out any light, by using earplugs, headphones, or a white noise machine to mask any noise, and by using a fan, an air conditioner, or a heater to regulate the temperature to your preference.
- Make your bed pleasant, cozy, and clean, by using a mattress, a pillow, a blanket, and a sheet that meet your comfort and support needs, and by changing and cleaning them often, to avoid any dust, dirt, or allergies from gathering.
- Make your bedroom a sleep-only zone, by eliminating or avoiding any things or activities that might distract or arouse you, such as TVs, laptops, phones, or work.

Adopt a peaceful nighttime ritual: Adopting a calming bedtime routine can assist you to quiet your body and mind, and notify your brain that it is time to sleep. Adopting a soothing sleep routine can also assist you in managing any tension, worry, or anxieties that may keep you awake at night. To develop a soothing sleep routine, you need to:

Mental turmoil

- Start your routine at least 30 minutes before your bedtime, and follow it regularly every night, including on weekends or vacations. You may use a reminder, an app, or a timer to assist you in staying to your schedule, and to avoid any delays or disruptions.
- Choose peaceful and delightful hobbies, such as reading a book, listening to soothing music, meditating, or breathing deeply. You may also employ aromatherapy, such as lavender or chamomile, to boost your relaxation and sleep quality.
- Avoid stimulating or stressful activities, such as watching TV, browsing the internet, checking your phone, or working. You may also avoid any emotional or heated talks, or any tough or crucial decisions, that may lead you to feel uncomfortable, worried, or furious.

Limit your exposure to blue light: Limiting your exposure to blue light will assist you in regulating your circadian rhythm, which is your natural sleep-wake cycle, and boost your melatonin levels, which is the hormone that governs your drowsiness and alertness. Limiting your exposure to blue light can also help you prevent any excitement or distraction that may interfere with your sleep. To decrease your exposure to blue light, you need to:

- Get adequate natural light exposure during the day, especially in the morning, by walking outside, opening your windows, or utilizing a light treatment device. This can enable you to enhance your mood, energy, and alertness, and to align your internal clock with the external light-dark cycle.
- Avoid artificial light exposure at night, especially from electronic gadgets, such as TVs, laptops, phones, or tablets, that create blue light, which can suppress your melatonin synthesis and interrupt your sleep. You can use blue light-blocking glasses, filters, or applications, to minimize the amount of blue light that hits your eyes, or you can switch off or dim your gadgets at least two hours before your bedtime.
- Watch what you eat and drink: Watching what you eat and drink will help you to prevent any discomfort or interruption that may impair your sleep quality and amount. Watching what you eat and drink may also enable you to optimize your nutrition and hydration, which can promote your

health and well-being. To watch what you eat and drink, you should:

- Avoid large or heavy meals, especially in the evening, since they can create indigestion, heartburn, or reflux, which can make it hard for you to go asleep or remain asleep. You may also avoid hot, fatty, or acidic foods that might irritate your stomach or esophagus, and increase your symptoms.
- Avoid coffee, alcohol, or nicotine, especially in the afternoon or evening, since they might excite your nervous system, and make it hard for you to fall asleep or remain asleep. You may also avoid any drinks that include sugar, artificial sweeteners, or additives, that might impact your blood sugar levels, and cause you to feel restless, jittery, or hungry.
- Drink enough water, but not too much, especially in the evening, since it can assist you to keep hydrated, and flush out any toxins or waste from your body. However, drinking too much water might lead you to wake up frequently to pee, which can interrupt your sleep cycle and your sleep quality.

- Exercise often, but not too close to your bedtime: Exercising regularly can assist you to improve your physical and mental health, and to boost your sleep quality and quantity. Exercising frequently can also assist you in lowering your stress, anxiety, and sadness, and boost your happiness, optimism, and well-being. To exercise frequently, you need to:

- Choose an exercise that you love and that meets your fitness level, such as walking, jogging, cycling, swimming, or yoga. You may also change your workout, and attempt new activities, to keep yourself motivated and engaged.
- Aim for at least 150 minutes of moderate-intensity or 75 minutes of high-intensity physical exercise each week, or a combination of both, according to the World Health Organization. However, you may vary the quantity according to your specific needs, tastes, and objectives.
- Avoid exercising too close to your bedtime, since it can boost your body temperature, heart rate, and cortisol levels, and make it hard for you to go asleep or remain asleep. You can exercise in the morning or afternoon, or at least three hours before your bedtime, to enable your body and mind to calm down and rest.

Manage your stress, anxiety, and worries: Managing your stress, anxiety, and worries can assist you to relax your body and mind, and to prevent or lessen any unpleasant emotions or thoughts that may keep you awake at night. Managing your stress, worry, and fears may also enable you to cope with any difficulties or obstacles that you have, and to enhance your mental and emotional health and well-being. To control your stress, anxiety, and worry, you need to:

- Identify and address the origins of your stress, worry, and fears, by utilizing problem-solving, coping, or relaxing tactics, such as setting priorities, delegating responsibilities, getting help, or meditating. You may also use cognitive restructuring or reframing strategies, such as the ones we explored in Chapter 5, to confront and modify your illogical, negative, or unhelpful beliefs, and to replace them with more reasonable, positive, or helpful ones.
- Express and release your tension, worry, and anxieties, by utilizing healthy and constructive outlets, such as talking to someone, writing in a diary, or indulging in a pastime. You may also utilize emotional regulation or management strategies, such as the ones we reviewed in Chapter 4, to recognize and describe your emotions, accept

Mental turmoil

and validate your feelings, and select and act on your emotions.
- Avoid or limit your exposure to stress, worry, and concerns, by setting boundaries, saying no, or taking pauses, when you feel overwhelmed or weary. You may also avoid or restrict any triggers or stimuli that can create or increase your stress, worry, or concerns, such as news, social media, or unpleasant individuals.

Sleep is a simple and effective exercise that you may employ to cultivate your calm and to obtain increased mental clarity. You may utilize it to relax and restore your body and mind and to integrate and consolidate your memories, emotions, and learning. You may also use it to manage your hormones, including cortisol and melatonin, which impact your mood, energy, and alertness.

Chapter 9

Disconnect to Reconnect: Digital Detox Strategies for a Quieter Mind

Technology, especially digital technology, such as cellphones, laptops, tablets, and social media, has become a vital part of our life. Technology may deliver various benefits, such as convenience, communication, information, entertainment, and education. However, technology may also offer numerous issues, such as distraction, addiction, worry, anxiety, and loneliness.

According to research by the Pew Research Center, 28% of American adults say they go online virtually continuously, while 45% say they go online many times a day. Moreover, according to a poll by the American Psychological Association, 65% of Americans think that regularly unplugging or taking a digital detox is crucial for their mental health, but just 28% of those who agree actually do so.

The continual and excessive use of technology can have detrimental impacts on your mental and emotional health, such as:

Impairing your attention and focus: Technology can impair your attention and focus, by generating various sources of distraction and stimulus, such as notifications, messages, emails, or news. Technology can also hamper your capacity to filter out extraneous information, and to transition between jobs quickly. Technology can also limit your attention span, and make you more prone to boredom, irritation, or annoyance.

Affecting your memory and learning: Technology may influence your memory and learning, by lessening your need and capacity to retain and recall knowledge, and by relying on external sources, such as search engines, applications, or gadgets. Technology can also influence your capacity to process and integrate information, and to build meaningful connections and relationships. Technology can also diminish your originality and curiosity, and make you more passive and shallow in your learning.

Altering your mood and emotions: Technology may influence your mood and emotions, by exposing you to a steady stream of good or negative stimuli, such as likes, comments, shares, or news. Technology can also alter your emotional control, and make you more reactive and impulsive in your answers. Technology may also impact your self-esteem and self-image, and make you more prone to social comparison, jealousy, or insecurity.

Disrupting your relationships and social skills: Technology may disrupt your relationships and social skills, by diminishing your face-to-face interactions and communication, and by boosting your online contacts and communication. Technology can also impair your social cues and empathy, and make you less conscious and sensitive to the feelings and needs of others. Technology may sometimes generate a sense of isolation and loneliness, and make you feel less connected and supported.

These negative consequences of technology might interfere with your mental clarity, and make you feel more confused, overwhelmed, or sad. Therefore, it is vital to balance your technology use and to disengage from technology regularly, to reconnect with yourself and others, and to obtain a quieter and clearer mind.

A digital detox is a period of time when you actively restrict or refrain from using technology, especially digital technology, such as smartphones, laptops, tablets, and social media. A digital detox can enable you to recover control over your technology use and restore your mental and emotional health and well-being.

In this chapter, we will cover some of the benefits and techniques of performing a digital detox, and some of the ideas and suggestions on how to make it effective and fun. We will also share some examples of digital detox activities that you may undertake, based on your interests, requirements, and goals.

The Benefits of a Digital Detox

A digital detox can have several benefits for your mental and emotional wellbeing, such as:

Improving your attention and concentration: A digital detox can enable you to enhance your attention and focus, by decreasing or removing the sources of distraction and stimulation, such as notifications, messages, emails, or news. A digital detox can also enable you to enhance your capacity to filter out extraneous information, and to transition between activities quickly. A digital detox can also boost your attention span, and make you more involved and interested in your activities.

Enhancing your memory and learning: A digital detox can enable you to boost your memory and learning, by increasing your demand and capacity to retain and recall knowledge, and by relying on your own sources, such as your brain, books, or people. A digital detox can also enable you to boost your capacity to digest and integrate information, and to build meaningful connections and relationships. A digital detox may also improve your creativity and curiosity, and make you more active and in-depth in your study.

Boosting your mood and emotions: A digital detox can enable you to increase your mood and emotions, by exposing you to a more balanced and realistic stream of stimuli, such as nature, art, or music. A digital detox can also enable you to enhance your emotional control and make you more contemplative and purposeful in your answers. A digital detox may also boost your self-esteem and self-image, and make you more confident and true in yourself.

Strengthening your relationships and social skills: A digital detox can enable you to enhance your relationships and social skills, by boosting your face-to-face contacts and communication, and by lowering your online interactions and communication. A digital detox can also enable you to strengthen your social signals and empathy and make you more aware and receptive to the feelings and needs of others. A digital detox may also provide a sense of connection and belonging, and make you feel more supported and cared for.

These benefits of a digital detox might boost your brain clarity, and make you feel more peaceful, clear, and cheerful. Therefore, it is good to attempt a digital detox and to feel the pleasant results for yourself.

How to Do a Digital Detox

There are various ways to undertake a digital detox, and you may select the ones that suit your interests, requirements, and goals. However, the core concepts of a digital detox remain the same, regardless of the approach or strategy. Here are some broad recommendations on how to undertake a digital detox:

make a clear and realistic objective: To conduct a digital detox, you need to make a clear and reasonable goal that specifies the duration, frequency, and breadth of your digital detox. For example, you can opt to perform a digital detox for a day, a week, or a month, or you might decide to do a digital detox once a week, once a month, or once a year. You can also elect to perform a digital detox for all or some of your devices or applications, such as your smartphone, your computer, your tablet, or your social media. You may use a planner, a calendar, or an app to help you create and track your objective, and to alter it gradually if required.

Prepare yourself and others: To undertake a digital detox, you need to prepare yourself and others, by informing and explaining your purpose, and by seeking and organizing their support and cooperation. For example, you can notify your family, friends, coworkers, or clients that you are conducting a digital detox, and why you are doing it. You can also urge them to appreciate and understand your decision and to avoid or minimize contacting you during your digital detox unless there is an emergency. You may also set up an auto-reply or a voicemail message, to let people know that you are conducting a digital detox, and when you will be back online.

unplug and reconnect: To complete a digital detox, you need to unplug from technology and reconnect with yourself and others, by engaging in activities that are important, fun, and gratifying. For example, you can disengage from technology, by turning off or silencing your gadgets or applications, or by putting them aside or out of sight. You may also reconnect with yourself and others, by engaging in hobbies, such as reading, writing, meditating, exercising, volunteering, learning, or socializing. You can use a list, a diary, or a notebook, to help you plan and document your activities, and to reflect on your experience.

Some Tips and Suggestions for a Successful and Enjoyable Digital Detox

Start slowly and gradually: To make your digital detox successful and pleasurable, you do not need to do too much or too fast. You may start with modest and incremental steps, such as completing a digital detox for an hour, a day, or a weekend, or conducting a digital detox for one device or app, such as your smartphone or your social network. You may also increase the duration, frequency, and scope of your digital detox gradually, as you feel more comfortable and competent. By starting softly and gradually, you can prevent withdrawal, worry, or frustration, and you can also build your habit and momentum.

find something you love: To make your digital detox successful and pleasurable, you need to find something that you enjoy and that matches your personality, interests, and goals. You may try with numerous hobbies and experiences, and find the ones that make you feel good, happy, and fulfilled. You may also diversify your hobbies and experiences, and try new things, to keep yourself motivated and interesting.

create reasonable and precise goals: To make your digital detox effective and pleasurable, you need to create realistic and explicit objectives that are reachable and quantifiable. You can utilize the SMART criteria, which stands for Specific, Measurable, Achievable, Relevant, and Time-bound, to create your expectations. For example, instead of expressing "I want to do a digital detox", you may say "I want to undertake a digital detox for one day, once a week, for the next month, and I anticipate feeling more peaceful, clear, and cheerful". By setting reasonable and clear objectives, you can measure your progress, celebrate your triumphs, and reward yourself for your efforts.

locate a companion or a group: To make your digital detox effective and fun, you may locate a partner or a group that can support and encourage you, and that can share your experience and delight. You can discover a partner or a group that has comparable or complementary objectives, tastes, and requirements, and that can give you feedback, guidance, or companionship. You may also join a class, a club, or an online community that can provide you with assistance, teaching, or inspiration. By finding a partner or a group, you may improve your accountability, dedication, and pleasure.

Be flexible and adaptable: To make your digital detox effective and pleasurable, you need to be flexible and adaptable and change your digital detox according to your circumstances, conditions, and requirements. You may be flexible and adaptive by having a backup plan, such as utilizing a landline, a radio, or a newspaper, in case of an emergency, or in case you need some information or amusement. You may also be flexible and adaptive by listening to your body and mind and respecting your boundaries, such as taking a break, or utilizing some technology when you feel too alone, bored, or nervous. By being flexible and adaptive, you can prevent or overcome challenges, and you can also prevent or lessen boredom, worry, or guilt.

Some Examples of Digital Detox Activities

Here are some examples of digital detox activities that you may do, depending on your interests, requirements, and goals:

Nature: Nature is one of the finest methods to disconnect from technology and reconnect with yourself and others, as it may give you beauty, peace, and harmony. You may appreciate nature by going for a stroll, a trek, a bike, or a picnic, in a park, a forest, a mountain, or a beach. You may also enjoy nature via gardening, camping, fishing, or birding, in your backyard, a farm, a lake, or a wildlife reserve. You may use your senses to appreciate and explore nature, such as sight, sound, smell, touch, or taste, and you can also use your imagination and creativity to create or find something new in nature, such as a flower, a rock, or a cloud.

Art: Art is another fantastic method to disengage from technology and to reconnect with yourself and others, since it may give you expression, inspiration, and joy. You can appreciate art by producing or making something, such as painting, sketching, sculpting, or knitting, using your hands, your tools, or your materials. You may also appreciate art by appreciating or learning anything, such as visiting a museum, a gallery, or a studio, or taking a lesson, a workshop, or a course, in any art form, such as music, dancing, or literature. You may use your emotions and ideas to express and explore art, such as happiness, sadness, or curiosity, and you can also utilize your abilities and talents to develop and enhance art, such as technique, style, or originality.

Volunteering: Volunteering is another fantastic method to disconnect from technology and reconnect with yourself and others, as it may offer you meaning, purpose, and value. You can volunteer by helping or serving someone or something, such as a person, an animal, or a cause that requires your aid, support, or advocacy. You may also volunteer by offering or contributing anything, such as your time, your money, or your resources, that can help someone or something, that deserves your generosity, appreciation, or acknowledgment. You may utilize your beliefs and interests to pick and pursue volunteering, such as compassion, justice, or education, and you can also use your talents and gifts to contribute and make a difference in volunteering, such as knowledge, skill, or talent.

These are some of the examples of digital detox activities that you may do, and that can enable you to detach from technology and reconnect with yourself and others. You may also come up with your own ideas, or you can mix and match different activities, to fit your interests, requirements, and ambitions. The idea is to discover something that makes you feel peaceful, clear, and cheerful, and that promotes your mental clarity and well-being.

Mental turmoil

A digital detox is a simple and effective exercise that you may take to cultivate your calm and obtain better mental clarity. You may use it to reclaim control over your technology use and to restore your mental and emotional health and well-being. You may also use it to reconnect with yourself and others and to enjoy the richness and complexity of life.

Part 3: Beyond the Steps: Maintaining Balance and Resilience

In the previous sections of this book, we have explored the actions and tactics that might assist you in obtaining mental clarity, such as cognitive restructuring, emotional regulation, mindfulness, gratitude, self-compassion, sleep hygiene, and digital detox. However, developing mental clarity is not a one-time event, but a continual process that demands continuing effort and adaptability. In this portion, we will discuss how to preserve balance and resilience in your life, and how to manage the inevitable changes and challenges that you will experience.

Balance and resilience are two connected ideas that are vital for your mental and emotional health and well-being. Balance is the condition of being in harmony with yourself and your surroundings, and having a sense of stability, control, and happiness in your life. Resilience is the ability to adapt successfully to adversity, trauma, stress, or change, and to emerge stronger, wiser, and more capable.

Balance and resilience are not set or static, but dynamic and fluid. They can change according to the situation, the person, and the time. They can also be impacted by various aspects, such as your personality, your values, your ambitions, your resources, and your support system. Therefore, balance and resilience are not something that you have or don't have, but something that you can grow and enhance.

How to Maintain Balance and Resilience

There are various strategies to preserve balance and resilience in your life, and you may select the ones that suit your tastes, requirements, and goals. However, the underlying concepts of balance and resilience remain the same, regardless of the approach or methodology. Here are some broad tips on how to maintain balance and resilience:

Know yourself: To preserve balance and resilience, you need to know yourself, and to be aware of your strengths, weaknesses, needs, wants, and limits. You may utilize self-assessment tools, such as personality tests, values inventories, or goal-setting worksheets, to help you discover and understand yourself better. You may also employ self-reflection tools, such as journaling, meditation, or feedback, to help you check and assess yourself periodically. By knowing yourself, you can make better choices and decisions, and you can also create realistic and explicit expectations and boundaries for yourself and others.

Manage your stress: To preserve balance and resilience, you need to manage your stress and prevent or lessen any negative impacts that stress can have on your physical, mental, and emotional health and well-being. You may employ stress management strategies, such as relaxation, breathing, or exercise, to help you calm your body and mind, and to relieve any tension or strain. You may also employ coping skills, such as problem-solving, positive thinking, or humor, to help you deal with any pressures or problems, and to find meaning, purpose, or worth in them. By controlling your stress, you may boost your mood, energy, and performance, and you can also avoid or overcome burnout, exhaustion, or disease.

cultivate your connections: To preserve balance and resilience, you need to cultivate your relationships, and to connect with individuals who can support, encourage, and inspire you. You may utilize communication skills, such as listening, expressing, or bargaining, to help you create and retain trust, respect, and understanding with others. You may also employ social skills, such as empathy, compassion, or appreciation, to help you appreciate and care for others, and to receive and provide support when required. By fostering your relationships, you may boost your happiness, optimism, and well-being, and you can also lessen your isolation, loneliness, or sadness.

explore your passions: To preserve balance and resilience, you need to explore your passions and engage in activities that are significant, fun, and rewarding for you. You may utilize your passions to drive and lead you and to express and discover yourself. You may also utilize your passions to challenge and grow yourself and to develop and improve your skills and talents. By pursuing your passions, you may boost your creativity, productivity, and performance, and you can also reach your goals, dreams, and potential.

Mental turmoil

Seek new experiences: To preserve balance and resilience, you need to seek new experiences and expose yourself to diverse circumstances, people, and viewpoints. You may utilize fresh experiences to learn and discover new things and to enhance and deepen your knowledge and understanding. You may also utilize new experiences to test and extend yourself and to adapt and adjust to change and uncertainty. By exploring new experiences, you may improve your curiosity, interest, and enthusiasm, and you can also develop your flexibility, adaptability, and resourcefulness.

Balance and resilience are simple and powerful principles that you can utilize to preserve your mental clarity, and to improve your mental and emotional health and well-being. You may utilize them to balance yourself and your surroundings and to adapt successfully to adversity, trauma, stress, or change. You may also utilize them to grow and better yourself and to gain more pleasure, contentment, and happiness in your life.

Chapter 10

Building Your Mental Fortress: Long-Term Strategies for Stress Management and Well-being

Building a solid and durable foundation for your mental clarity is like building a fortress for your mind, that can shield you from the external and internal dangers that might weaken your mental clarity, such as stress, worry, negativity, or confusion. Building a fortress for your mind may also enable you to face and conquer the obstacles and possibilities that can boost your mental clarity, such as learning, growth, or change.

Mental turmoil

Let us explore some of the long-term tactics that can enable you to create a fortress for your mind, and to manage your stress and well-being in the long run. These tactics are:

Develop a growth mindset: Developing a growth mindset can assist you to create a fortress for your mind, by helping you to perceive your abilities, skills, and talents as pliable and improvable, rather than fixed and immutable. Developing a growth mindset can also assist you in perceiving your problems, failures, and feedback as opportunities and incentives for learning and progress, rather than as threats and impediments to success and achievement.

A growth mindset can assist you to manage your stress and well-being in the long term, by improving your motivation, confidence, and resilience, and by lowering your fear, worry, and frustration. A growth mindset may also enable you to reach your goals, aspirations, and potential, and to boost your mental clarity and well-being.

To establish a growth mindset, you need to:

Mental turmoil

1.Recognize and question your fixed mentality, which is the notion that your abilities, skills, and talents are intrinsic and unchanging and that your success and achievement depend on them. You may use cognitive restructuring strategies, such as the ones we described in Chapter 2, to recognize and modify your fixed mindset thinking, such as "I can't do this", "I'm not good enough", or "This is too hard".

2.Cultivate and reinforce your growth mindset, which is the concept that your abilities, skills, and talents can be developed and enhanced through effort, practice, and feedback. You may use positive thinking tactics, such as the ones we reviewed in Chapter 3, to develop and validate your growth mindset concepts, such as "I can learn this", "I can better myself", or "This is a problem that I can conquer".

3.Apply and practice your growth mindset, by creating realistic and precise objectives, by seeking and embracing challenges, by enduring and persevering in the face of adversity, by seeking and accepting criticism, and by celebrating and learning from your accomplishments and disappointments.

construct a strong support system: Building a strong support system may allow you to construct a fortress for your mind, by giving you the people and resources that can support, encourage, and inspire you. Building a solid support system may also enable you to cope with and overcome the pressures and challenges that might influence your mental clarity and well-being.

A support system can assist you to manage your stress and well-being in the long term, by improving your happiness, optimism, and well-being, and by lowering your isolation, loneliness, and sadness. A support system may also enable you to realize your goals, objectives, and potential, and to boost your mental clarity and well-being.

To develop a strong support system, you need to:

1. Identify and connect with your support system, which might include your family, friends, coworkers, mentors, or professionals, who can provide you with emotional, practical, informational, or motivational help. You may utilize communication skills, such as the ones we reviewed in Chapter 6, to create and maintain trust, respect, and understanding with your support system, and to

communicate and share your feelings, ideas, and needs with them.

2. Seek and accept support from your support system, by reaching out to them when you need help, advice, or direction, and by being open and responsive to their criticism, suggestions, or assistance. You may also utilize social skills, such as the ones we addressed in Chapter 7, to appreciate and care for your support system, and to provide and accept aid when required.

3. Expand and diversify your support system, by finding and joining new groups, communities, or networks that might offer you alternative viewpoints, experiences, or possibilities. You may also utilize networking abilities, such as the ones we reviewed in Chapter 8, to introduce yourself, to create a good impression, and to develop and cultivate connections with new individuals.

Practice self-care and wellness: Practicing self-care and wellness will enable you to construct a fortress for your mind, by taking care of your physical, mental, and emotional health and well-being. Practicing self-care and wellness can also assist you in preventing or decreasing any diseases or injuries that might damage your mental clarity and well-being.

Mental turmoil

Self-care and wellness may assist you to manage your stress and well-being in the long term, by boosting your energy, vitality, and performance, and by minimizing your weariness, pain, and discomfort. Self-care and wellness may also enable you to reach your goals, objectives, and potential, and to boost your mental clarity and well-being.

To practice self-care and wellbeing, you need to:

1. Eat well and drink well, by choosing healthy and balanced meals and drinks that can offer you the vitamins, minerals, and antioxidants that can promote your health and well-being. You can also avoid or restrict meals and drinks that can impair your health and well-being, such as junk food, processed food, or alcohol. You may utilize nutrition and hydration guidelines, such as the ones offered by the World Health Organization, to help you plan and manage your food and hydration.

2. Sleep well and rest well, by maintaining a regular and consistent sleep schedule, establishing a pleasant and favorable resting environment, and adopting a soothing nighttime practice, as we mentioned in Chapter 9. You may also avoid or

minimize anything that can interrupt or disturb your sleep, such as coffee, nicotine, or blue light. You may employ sleep hygiene advice and ideas, such as the ones offered by the National Sleep Foundation, to help you improve your sleep quality and quantity.

3. Exercise well and move well, by engaging in physical activities that can enhance your cardiovascular, muscular, and skeletal health and well-being, such as walking, jogging, cycling, swimming, or yoga. You can also prevent or restrict physical inactivity or sedentary behavior, such as sitting, lying, or watching TV. You may utilize physical activity guidelines, such as the ones offered by the World Health Organization, to help you plan and track your exercise and movement.

4. Relax properly and have fun, by engaging in activities that can lower your tension, anxiety, and negativity, and that can promote your happiness, optimism, and well-being, such as meditation, breathing, or laughing. You can also indulge in activities that can offer you happiness, pleasure, and satisfaction, such as hobbies, games, or entertainment. You may utilize relaxation and fun recommendations, such as the ones published by the American Psychological Association, to help you plan and track your relaxation and fun activities.

5. Take care of yourself and respect yourself, by being kind, compassionate, and forgiving toward yourself, especially when you are hurting or struggling, as we described in Chapter 7. You may also be polite, thankful, and proud of yourself, and appreciate your characteristics, skills, and successes. You may utilize self-care and self-love advice and recommendations, such as the ones supplied by the Mayo Clinic, to help you enhance your self-care and self-love.

Learn new skills and knowledge: Learning new skills and knowledge may enable you to create a fortress for your mind, by increasing and enhancing your cognitive talents and capabilities, such as memory, reasoning, problem-solving, and decision-making. Learning new skills and information may also allow you to explore and discover new things, and to fulfill your curiosity and enthusiasm.

Learning new skills and information can assist you to manage your stress and well-being in the long term, by boosting your competence, confidence, and resilience, and by lowering your boredom, stagnation, and frustration. Learning new skills and information may also enable you to reach your goals, aspirations, and potential, and to boost your mental clarity and well-being.

Mental turmoil

To develop new skills and information, you need to:

1. Identify and pick your learning goals, which might be connected to your personal or professional interests, passions, or requirements. You may utilize goal-setting approaches, such as the ones we reviewed in Chapter 3, to help you define realistic and precise learning goals, and to track and assess your progress and outcomes.

2. Seek and access your learning resources, which can include books, articles, podcasts, videos, courses, seminars, or mentors, that can offer you the knowledge, instruction, or direction that you need. You may use research and assessment approaches, such as the ones we described in Chapter 4, to help you locate and pick the finest and most dependable learning materials for your learning goals.

3. Apply and apply your learning, by utilizing active and effective learning tactics, such as summarizing, questioning, explaining, or testing, that can enable you to process and consolidate your learning, and to make meaningful connections and associations. You may also utilize feedback and reflection strategies, such as the ones we described in Chapter 5, to help you monitor and assess your learning, and to

identify and address your strengths and shortcomings.

These are some of the long-term tactics that can enable you to create a fortress for your mind and manage your stress and well-being in the long run. You may also employ the practices that we have addressed in the previous chapters, including cognitive restructuring, emotional regulation, mindfulness, gratitude, self-compassion, sleep hygiene, and digital detox, to support and strengthen your long-term plans. The goal is to uncover what works for you, and then to practice and apply it consistently and efficiently.

Building a fortress for your mind is a simple and powerful notion that you can utilize to preserve your mental clarity, and to improve your mental and emotional health and well-being. You may use it to shield yourself against external and internal hazards that might weaken your mental clarity, such as stress, worry, negativity, or confusion. You may also utilize it to empower yourself to meet and conquer the obstacles and opportunities that can boost your mental clarity, such as learning, growth, or change. You may also utilize it to grow and better yourself and to gain more pleasure, contentment, and happiness in your life.

Mental turmoil

Conclusion

We have reached the conclusion of this book, and we hope that you have found it helpful and informative. We have shared with you the six easy actions that may assist you in washing off your mental turbulence and cutting down your stress, discomfort, and too much pondering. These steps are:

1. Cognitive restructuring: How to transform your illogical, negative, or harmful thoughts, and to replace them with more reasonable, positive, or useful ones.

2. Emotional regulation: How to recognize, classify, accept, and regulate your emotions, and to select and act on them intelligently and effectively.

3. Mindfulness: Mindfulness is the practice of being present, aware, and attentive to one's experiences, as well as the ability to watch and accept such experiences without reacting or passing judgment on them.

4. Gratitude: How to recognize and show gratitude for what you have, as well as how to concentrate on the positive parts of your life, is what is referred to as gratitude.

5.   Self-compassion: How to be kind, compassionate, and forgiving toward oneself, especially when you are hurting or struggling.

6. Sleep hygiene: How to increase your sleep quality and quantity, and to optimize your routines and behaviors that support excellent sleep.

We have also addressed how to preserve balance and resilience in your life, and how to create a fortress for your mind, by employing certain long-term techniques, such as:

1. Developing a growth mindset: How to perceive your abilities, skills, and talents as flexible and improvable, and to regard your difficulties, failures, and criticism as chances and incentives for learning and progress.

2. Building a solid support system: How to connect with those who can support, encourage, and inspire you, and to cope with and overcome the pressures and obstacles that can influence your mental clarity and well-being.

3. Practicing self-care and wellness: How to take care of your physical, mental, and emotional health and well-being, and to prevent or decrease any diseases or injuries that might influence your mental clarity and well-being.

4. Learning new skills and knowledge: How to extend and enrich your cognitive powers and capacities, explore and find new things, and fulfill your curiosity and interest.

I hope that by following these methods and tactics, you will be able to attain better mental clarity and enhance your mental and emotional health and well-being. I hope that you will be able to wipe off your mental turbulence and cut down your tensity, anxiety, and too much pondering. I hope that you will be able to live a more peaceful, clear, and joyful life.

I also want to thank you for picking this book, and for trusting us with your journey. I appreciate your time, attention, and criticism, and I hope that you have enjoyed reading this book as much as I have loved creating it. I wish you all the best, and I hope to hear from you soon. You have the power and the capacity to wipe off your mental anguish and acquire better mental clarity. You simply need to take the first step, and I'm here to support you along the road. Thank you, and farewell.